A Victorian Visit to
with excursions to Winchelsea, Rye, Battle and Bexhill

In the late 19th century, Britain's railway network was expanding rapidly and Sussex was particularly well served. Its coastal resorts were ideally located for day visitors from London and easily accessible to tourists from further afield. Hastings and its more genteel neighbour, St. Leonards, offered two different experiences in one visit, the former, 'unimproved and quaint', the latter, 'modern and fashionable'.

Detailed guide-books were available to help tourists make the most of their visit to Sussex, with chapters on history, geology, weather, where to stay and places of interest .... in fact, just about everything they could want or need to know. This booklet reproduces text from 'Black's Guide to Sussex', published in 1896, relating to Hastings and the surrounding area.

It is in two parts. The first is a history and general description of Sussex and the second, a fascinating exploration of Hastings, plus descriptions of excursions to the surrounding towns and smaller villages. A few pages are, of course, devoted to the Battle of Hastings but, as this booklet shows, there is far more history in these few square miles, than the events of 1066 alone, world-changing as they were.

The original guide-book has some 'foxing' (brown, age-related stains) and these appear on the pages of this booklet as dark marks and patches. The ten photographs date from the 1880s to the 1920s and are from the Keasbury-Gordon Photograph Archive. The one of the

German U-Boat on Hastings beach in April 1919, is particularly interesting.

The text is remarkably detailed and enables us to travel back in time to visit this historically important area of southern England. I hope you enjoy the journey.

Andrew Gill

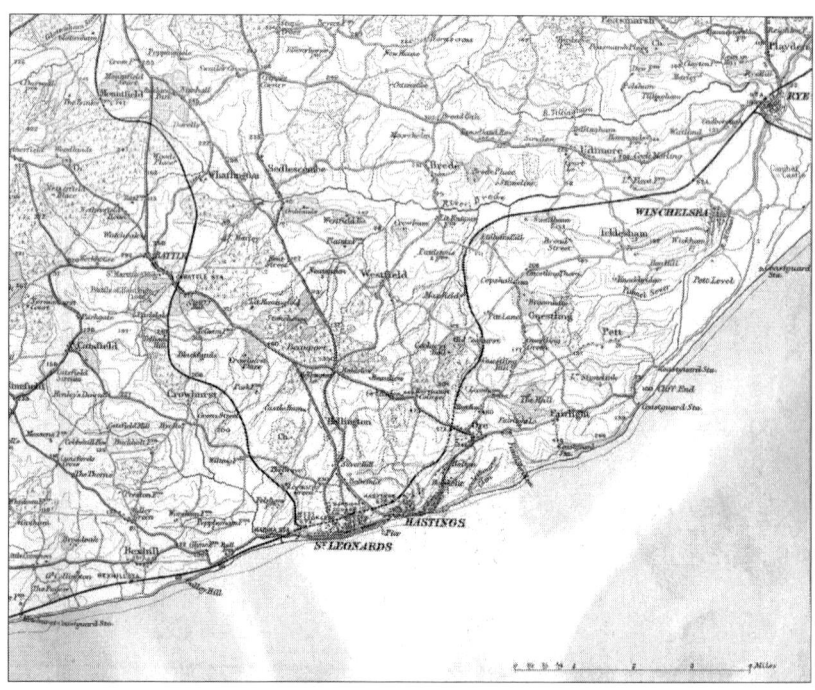

Road and rail links in 1896

The Kicking Donkey, Hill Street, Hastings

INTRODUCTION

The county of Sussex consists of an oblong territory, stretching along the southern coast of England, bounded on the west by Hampshire; on the north, north-east, and east by Surrey and Kent. The line of its coast, following the indentations, is nearly 90 miles long; the extreme length of the county in a straight line, from Ladyholt Park on the west, to the end of Kent Ditch on the east, is 76 miles; the extreme breadth, in a cross line from Tunbridge Wells on the north to Beachy Head on the south, 27 miles. It contains 933,269 acres, and is inhabited by a population which, according to the census of 1891, amounted to 550,446.

The whole district is divided into 6 rapes, 73 hundreds, and 312 civil parishes, containing 7 municipal boroughs, viz. Arundel, Chichester, Hastings, and Rye (by ancient title), Brighton (incorporated 1854), Lewes (1881), and Eastbourne (1883). Winchelsea, Seaford, Pevensey, and Midhurst were unreformed corporations existing under old charters; the first governed by a mayor and the latter three by bailiffs, but their privileges have been abolished. By the Redistribution of Seats Bill (1885) the parliamentary representation of Sussex is divided among 9 members—6 from rural constituencies, 2 from the borough of Brighton, and 1 from that of Hastings. But before the Reform Bill of 1832, Sussex returned no less than 28 members, and contained several "rotten" boroughs.

The *rape* is a division peculiar to Sussex, and not found in any other English county. The origin of the term has caused much discussion, but it is probably derived from the Icelandic *hreppr*, signifying land divided by a rope. There is no evidence of its existence before the Conquest, and it was doubtless introduced by the Normans, as it is first mentioned in the *Domesday Survey*. The rapes are Hastings, Pevensey, and Lewes in East Sussex, and Bramber, Arundel, and Chichester in West Sussex, their boundaries extending from the northern limit of the county to the coast. Each formerly enclosed one of the six military high roads to Normandy, and contained a castle, situate on a river or close to the sea.

Ecclesiastically the county is coextensive with the diocese of Chichester, subdivided into the archdeaconries and 11 rural deaneries of Lewes and Chichester. There are two County Councils, for East and West Sussex.

Physical Aspects.—The county is made up of two natural divisions very differently characterised, the coast and the Wealden district, lying south and north respectively. The coast is shut in by the South Downs, keeping, for the most part, parallel with the sea, a few miles behind it, till they end at the bold promontory of Beachy Head. This stretch of heights, between 40 and 50 miles long, broken here and there into blocks by the river valleys, has an average height of 500 feet, but at some points they swell up to over 800 feet. Ditchling Beacon (813 feet) is commonly spoken of as the highest point; but the latest *Ordnance Survey* gives a few feet more to Linch Ball, near the Hampshire border.

INTRODUCTION

The beauty of these "soft bosomy eminences" is quite their own. They have been compared to green waves of land copying its neighbour, the sea; and Mr. Harrison Ainsworth is not the only writer who has risen into enthusiasm over them. "No breeze so fresh and invigorating as that of these Sussex Downs; no turf so springy to the foot as their soft greensward! A flock of larks flies past us, and a cloud of mingled rooks and starlings wheels overhead. Mark yon little T-shaped cuttings on the slope below us—those are the snares set by the shepherds for the delicious wheat-ear, our English ortolan. The fairies still haunt this spot, and hold their midnight revels upon it, as yon dark green rings testify. The common folk hereabouts term the good people 'Pharisees,' and style these emerald circles 'hay tracks.' Why, we care not to inquire. Enough for us, the fairies are not altogether gone. A smooth soft carpet is here spread out for Oberon and Titania, and their attendant elves, to dance upon by moonlight; and there is no lack of mushrooms to form tables for 'Puck's banquets.'"

Even Harrison Ainsworth admits—though Gilbert White does not—that the South Downs want boldness and grandeur. To some their gentle softness has an effect of monotony; and, perhaps, one must grow familiar with them fully to enter into their peculiar charms, not as generally relished as the flavour of their mutton. One hill is often so like another that the stranger may easily go astray for want of landmarks to guide him to the scattered villages lying hidden in cup-like hollows. Thick weather here might make a real danger for bewildered wanderers, who in such a case are advised to orient themselves by noting the inclination of any timber exposed to the prevalent south-west winds, and how its sheltered side is more likely to be stained by lichen.

As a rule, the Downs themselves have a bolder face to the north, while they slope more gently on the sea-side, where the flat strip at their foot has suffered much from incursions of the waves. The site of the ancient cathedral of Selsey is now a mile out at sea. Between 1292 and 1340 A.D. upwards of 5500 acres were submerged. In the early part of the 14th century Pagham Harbour was formed by a sudden irruption of the sea, devastating 2700 acres, which recently have been reclaimed and again brought under cultivation. There is reason for believing that the whole coast-line of the county has been slightly raised in the last 800 years (possibly by earthquake shock), as the large estuaries at the river mouths no longer exist, and the archipelago of knolls round Pevensey (*eye* signifies "island") have only a slight elevation above the neighbouring marsh land.

Upon the north edge of the county, facing the Downs, runs more irregularly a sandy and well-wooded range of heights, known as the Forest Ridge, which turns southward beyond Tunbridge Wells, reaching the coast at Fairlight, near Hastings. Almost all the extent of this ridge offers beautiful scenery of a more varied type. The broken plain between, often rising into picturesque heights, was once thickly covered by forests, as its name of *Weald* implies. Here, till the 17th century, were the great ironworks of England, now transferred to the neighbourhood of coal-fields. The once famed Wealden forests, however, are not yet exhausted; considerable patches of them still remain, often as ornaments of the lordly parks forming such a frequent feature in Sussex, which contains no less than four ducal seats, and many others about which art has vied with nature to please the eye. There are few parts of England that make up a richer picture than the Weald of Sussex, with its mingled display of hill and dale, rich meadows, and wild commons, weathered cottages and noble mansions, backed by fine foliage and bold eminences.

In one kind of scenery the county is deficient. The rivers are short, and for the most part rather prosaic in their quiet course, generally southward. The least unimportant are the two Rothers, the Arun, the Adur, the Ouse, the Cuckmere, and the upper waters of the Medway.

Geology.—A great portion of the county is occupied by the Chalk formation, of which the South Downs are almost entirely composed. Firestone is found in the west, and Steyning is built upon it. At the base of the Downs the Greensand crops up, but is of small extent. The Wealden formations occupy nearly all the inland district of the county, and in these occurs the ironstone from which iron was extracted. Sussex was at one time the centre of the English iron manufacture; before 1653 there were 42 iron forges or mills (reduced to 18 before 1667) and 27 furnaces (reduced to 11 before 1664), which employed 50,000 men and furnished the main supply of ordnance for the national defence. The last forge at Ashburnham was not extinguished until 1809. Between 1872 and 1876 boring was carried on at Netherfield, near Battle, with the object of discovering what beds were below the Wealden, and if possible of reaching the Palæozoic rocks, which at Kentish Town, Harwich, Ostend, and Calais had been found at a depth of about 1000 feet below the sea-level. Some slight hope was entertained of the occurrence of Coal Measures, as in the

INTRODUCTION

Boulonnais the Carboniferous Limestone, where last seen, dips south. The boring was continued to a depth of 1905 feet, the Oxford Clay being reached. The chief result was the discovery of the unusual thickness of the Kimmeridge Clay, which began at 275 feet from the surface and continued to a depth of about 1469 feet. The most practical result was the finding of thick beds of gypsum (at about 160 feet), which were before unknown in the Weald, and are now worked at Netherfield. From Beachy Head to Selsey Bill there lies, south of the Downs, a low and level tract belonging to the Tertiary period, of which there is no such record at any other place in England. The towns of Hove, Worthing, Littlehampton, Bognor, etc., are built on gravel, sand, and loam of the Post-Pliocene or Pleistocene series, which superficial beds overlie the Eocene series in patches and contain a large fossil fauna. Remains of the mammoth occur in the mud deposit (or *Lutraria* clay) of this district, and the Chichester Museum contains the greater portion of a fine skeleton of the *Elephas antiquus* obtained off Selsey Bill. Of the British Quaternary fossils 45 are peculiar to Selsey, and 20 others probably find here their earliest place in British geological history. The Bracklesham beds occur at the bay of that name, their main divisions extending from Wittering on the west to the Barn Rocks, east of Selsey Bill, a distance of 7 miles. They are full of fossil shells, particularly nummulitic.

Flora.—An analysis of the flora of the county was placed before the British Association in 1872 by Mr. W. B. Hemsley (*Report*, 1872, p. 128), who stated the total number of indigenous plants to be 1000, to which 59 introduced species must be added. The most interesting features of the flora are the number of species to the county area, the species peculiar to certain formations, viz. the Chalk (56), maritime species (76), and the rare species, especially of the Atlantic and Scottish types. Amongst the rarer marsh plants are *Isnardia palustris, Scirpus triqueter, S. carinatus, Pyrola media, Habeneria albida, Festuca sylvatica* of the "Scottish" type of Watson; this last is not found in adjoining counties. A prominent feature of the Wealden flora is the extent of heath land and the large size the heath attains.

History and Antiquities. — The earliest known settlers here were the Celtic tribes, whose memorials are found in the hill-forts of Mount Caburn, Hollingbury, White Hawk, Ditchling Beacon, Devil's Dyke, Chanctonbury Hill, Cissbury, etc., the latter being a great factory for flint implements. They gave the names to the rivers. Little is, however, known of them beyond the fact that they had a distinct coinage some two centuries before the Roman invasion,—a coarse imitation of the Greek *stater* of Philip II. of Macedon. These coins have been found in various parts of Sussex. At the time of Cæsar's landing (55 B.C.) the Belgic tribe of the Regni inhabited the county and had their capital at Regnum (Chichester). Sir G. B. Airy fixed on Pevensey as the place of Cæsar's landings in 55 and 54 B.C.; this is, however, much disputed, and opinion generally puts the landing near Deal. A few years after this Sussex appears to have formed part of the kingdom of Commius, a British chieftain, and upon his death seems to have been allotted to his son Tincommius. These two are the only British rulers of the county whose coins have been found.

Upon the conquest of Britain under Claudius, the Romans found a ready tool in a king named Cogidubnus, mentioned by Tacitus, who was created imperial legate,

INTRODUCTION

and may probably be identified with the king of that name mentioned in the celebrated inscription on the temple of Neptune and Minerva found at Chichester. Sussex was conquered prior to the reign of Vespasian, and Major-General Pitt-Rivers suggests that the hill-fort of Mount Caburn may have been one of the twenty *oppida* Suetonius states to have been reduced by that emperor. Roman settlements became numerous in the county, and villas sprang up, the remains of which are still occasionally found, the chief being that at Bignor, near Stane Street, the Roman road connecting Chichester with London, still partly traceable. A fortress was erected at Anderida (Pevensey), and there was another town named Mutuantonis, which is thought to be Lewes; but it may have been situated farther west than Lewes, perhaps at Littlehampton.

Sussex was the first county invaded by the Saxons, who in 477 landed under Ælle at Keynor, near Chichester. After fourteen years of struggle they reached the point where the South Downs abut on the sea at Beachy Head, and in 491, as the *Saxon Chronicle* grimly records, "Ælle and Cissa beset Andredes-ceaster (Anderida), and slew all that were therein, nor was there a Briton left there any more." This resulted in the formation of a distinct kingdom of South Saxons, whence its name of *Sussex*. The subjugation of the county was very complete, for it is still one of the most thoroughly Saxon counties in England, and its inhabitants, speech, place-names, customs, etc., are almost entirely Saxon.

The next important event in the history of the county was the landing of William of Normandy (28th September 1066), followed by the battle of Senlac or Hastings (14th October 1066). The Conqueror erected on the battlefield an abbey dedicated to St. Martin, but this was not completed until after his death. Then came the great battle of Lewes between Henry III. and the barons under Simon de Montfort in 1264, which "wiped out the stain—if stain it were—of Senlac." Other important events have been the rebellion of Jack Cade in 1450, which received substantial support in East Sussex, and the naval engagement fought off Beachy Head in 1690, in which the English and Dutch fleets combined were defeated by the French. Charles II. in his flight after the battle of Worcester escaped in 1651 from Shoreham in a fishing-boat.

The foremost place amongst the illustrious natives of Sussex must be assigned to Shelley the poet. As statesmen we have John Selden and Richard Cobden, and as eminent ecclesiastics Archbishops Frewen and William Juxon, also Archdeacon Hare. Its poets include Thomas Otway, Thomas Sackville (afterwards Earl of Dorset), and John Fletcher. Among its antiquaries we find Sir William Burrell, John Elliot, Rev. Thomas W. Horsfield, Mark Antony Lower, Dr. Mantell (geologist), and Dr. Richard Russell (founder of modern Brighton).

Dialect.—A large number of Saxon words are still retained and pronounced in the old style; thus *gate* becomes *ge-at*. The letter *a* is very broad in all words, as if followed by *u*, and in fact converts words of one syllable into words of two, as *faüs* (face), *taüst* (taste), etc. Again, *a* before double *d* becomes *ar*, as *arder* and *larder* for *adder* and *ladder*; *oi* is like a long *i*, as *spile* (spoil), *intment* (ointment); an *e* is substituted for *a* in such words as *rag*, *flag*, etc. The French refugees in the 16th and 17th centuries introduced many words which are still in common use: a Sussex woman when unprepared to receive visitors says she is in *dishabille* (déshabillé, undress); if her child is unwell it looks *pekid* (piqué), if fretful is a little *peter-grievous* (petit-grief); she cooks with a *broach* (broche, a spit), and talks of *coasts* (coste, Old French) or ribs of meat, etc. There is an excellent *Dictionary of the Sussex Dialect*, by the Rev. W. D. Parish. As the names occur, we have pointed out local peculiarities of pronunciation that puzzle a stranger.

Climate.—The two districts of Sussex show a considerable contrast of climate—the Weald wetter and more in extremes, while the coast has greater equability and dryness, the annual rainfall here being 10 inches less than north of the Downs. Sussex, above all other parts of the English coast, seems to unite the two qualities of brightness and bracingness; certainly there is none within easy reach of London that enjoys such an amount of winter sunshine along with a tonic air where the cold is usually tempered, yet not to the relaxing mildness of our south-western resorts, with which Hastings alone may vie in this respect by its sheltered situation. All along the Sussex coast, then, there have sprung up a row of the most flourishing watering-places in the kingdom, Brighton the chief of them; and this, though the shore is far from beautiful or grand, unless at a few points, like Fairlight and Beachy Head.

To these crowded resorts and their vicinity we have given most space, on our principle of the greatest good of the greatest number. But we have not failed to guide our readers about the more numerous if less frequented centres of the northern district; and we believe that no place of note has been left unmentioned, at least in outline. Some lovely parts of the county are so little visited that, in the interest of the majority, we are conscious of not having done them justice. Still, whoever follows up all our more or less detailed indications, might say, as truly as Tennyson's *Harold*, "I know all Sussex!"

Railways.—The traversing of this county, which active pedestrians and cyclists can cross at a stretch, is facilitated by numerous railway lines, not to speak of the driving trips and excursion steamers plying in summer from places like Brighton and Hastings. In each section we have been careful to show the communications and opportunities for getting about. On its west and east sides, respectively, Sussex is touched by branches of the London and South-Western and of the South-Eastern Railway systems. But it mainly depends on the London, Brighton, and South Coast Railway, which, throughout nearly the whole county, has a monopoly of the traffic on its several lines and branches. There is no lack of trains on these, especially in the summer season; and by certain of them advantage can be taken of cheap fares, for which the Company's programmes may be studied. On the other hand, complaints are often made of unpunctuality, and sometimes of incivility on the part of porters, perhaps spoiled by the abundant "tips" of the great watering-places.

Hostelries here are of all sorts, from the palatial hotels of Brighton and Eastbourne to the unpretentious village inns, which often offer quite as much real comfort to travellers of simple tastes.

HASTINGS

THERE are two railway routes from London to Hastings, which have the advantage, for the public, of belonging to opposing companies. The London, Brighton, and South Coast Railway runs on from Polegate Junction, having taken up at Lewes the traffic from Brighton and Portsmouth. The London and South Eastern Railway reaches Hastings more directly through Tunbridge Wells, some of its express trains doing the distance in about two hours. The fares are the same (14s., 10s., 5s. 0$\frac{1}{2}$d.), and joint return tickets are issued available by either railway. As both these lines are to serve us in our excursions from Hastings, no more need be said about them at present.

HASTINGS AND ST. LEONARDS

Hotels: (almost all on the sea front, and arranged in order from west to east). In St. Leonards: *Sussex, Royal Victoria, Royal Saxon.* Beyond Warrior Square: *Eversfield, Alexandra, Grand, Palace* (C.), *Albany, Queen's.* These are the most expensive; the rest, in Hastings proper, are to some extent commercial houses: *Castle, Royal Oak, Royal Marine, Royal Albion.* The *Waverley* (C.) and smaller Temperance Hotels in Havelock Road, near the station.

Private Hotels: *The Edinburgh, Gifford's, Warrior House.* Except perhaps in holding a licence, these are hardly to be distinguished from the Boarding-houses of all sorts whose name here is legion. We can mention only a few. In St. Leonards: *Warrior Mansion, Bentley House, Lonsdale, Eversfield Mansion, Eversfield House, Drayton House, Stafford House,* with many others in and about Warrior Square. In Hastings: (as a rule less expensive) *Gildersleeve's, Sandringham, Kent House, Abbotsford House, Cornwallis House, Stanley House* (with baths). The *Hydropathic Establishment* (licensed) in the old London Road.

There are three railway stations here. Both the London, Brighton, and South Coast Railway and the London and South Eastern Railway stop

Hastings Railway Station

HASTINGS AND ST. LEONARDS

first at *West Marina*, or "Bo-Peep" station for the extreme west of St. Leonards, then at *Warrior Square* for the centre of the whole place; and their joint Terminus is above the busiest part of Hastings, whence the London and South Eastern Railway trains leave for Rye and other points of the coast eastward.

These two watering-places are practically one, and by their united attractions make up what many judge by far the most attractive resort in this corner of England. St. Leonards is modern, uniform, fashionable, the west end, both literally and figuratively, of Hastings. Hastings, though rapidly modernising, has still many nooks of ancient picturesqueness to show, and no "improvements" can spoil the advantages of its situation. The chief season in St. Leonards is winter; in summer rather Hastings is crowded with not too Vere-de-Vere-like relays of visitors, especially during the August week of regattas and other festivities, which has lately made the experiment of calling itself a "Carnival." Both towns have all the year round a fair share of guests as well as permanent residents, bringing the population up to over 60,000. Where the one begins and the other ends, it is hard to say. The absurd arch which used to mark the boundary has been removed, and the tendency is for houses on the front as far as Hastings Pier to rank themselves in St. Leonards as more genteel; but perhaps the spacious opening of Warrior Square makes the best division. The whole sea front is now continuous, forming a parade nearly 3 miles long, lit throughout by electric light.

Long before it became a health resort, Hastings was a place of considerable note, a settlement probably of the Saxon Hæstingas. In Edward the Confessor's time, it was an important seaport, with numerous ships and sailors, entitling it to rank chief among the Cinque Ports, though now its fleet of fishing boats are registered as hailing from the Port of Rye. Previous to this, the town seems to have lain more southward, so that the sea now conceals its earliest site. Then there came a day, that 28th of September 1066, so memorable through all history, when a mighty armament made its appearance in Pevensey Bay, pouring out countless thousands of warriors and archers and artificers, at, as near as we can tell, the little village of Bulverhythe, slightly westward of St. Leonards. When this great fleet was emptied, and his army covered the banks before him, their leader sprang from his boat, and in leaping, fell flat upon the sand. The countenances of his soldiers were gloomy as they saw his tall form lying prostrate; they regarded it as an evil omen, and a murmur immediately rose among them; but the "Conqueror" started up, with his hands clutched full of the sand—"What now! does that astonish you? I have taken seisin of this land with my hands, and, by the splendour of God, as far as it extends it is ours!" Joyous acclamations welcomed that view of the case. A stone named "the Conqueror's Table," from a tradition that William dined on it immediately he landed, was said to have marked the spot where this scene occurred. It has now been removed to the St. Leonards Gardens.

In spite of its privileges, much extended by Edward I. for maritime services rendered to the Crown, Hastings came to share the decay of neighbouring towns, ill-treated by the sea. In Elizabeth's reign the harbour was destroyed through the violence of a storm; and though from time to time efforts were made to reconstruct it, they proved unsuccessful. After the destruction of its pier, the port naturally declined, until at last it had sunk into a mere fishing village. But when, towards the latter part of the last century, Dr. Baillie turned the tide of popularity towards it as a watering-place, Hastings began steadily to increase with the influx of visitors, and with the enlargement of the old town by many new buildings and houses. These were speedily rivalled by the plans of Mr. Decimus Burton, to whom St. Leonards owes its architecturally imposing air.

Among distinguished sojourners at Hastings have been Louis Napoleon and Louis Philippe; and Sir Cloudesley Shovel and Titus Oates are two natives of it, who in very different ways achieved fame. Lord Byron and Charles Lamb have left records of their stay here. The latter for his part tells us it was "dreary penance," that there is "no sense of home at Hastings," and he showers abuse plentifully upon it, as he does upon Brighton and Eastbourne. But Campbell was subject to the same penance for five years; and that he thought very differently is apparent in his lines on the view from St. Leonards and his "Address to the Sea," which were written here.

Of late years, the town has shown a tendency to grow backwards for miles upon the spurs of hill which here run down to the shore, and along the enclosed valleys, whose course is sometimes so crooked as to make the geography of the place a puzzle to an idle explorer, who, after reaching what seems a truly rural nook, goes on to find himself brought up again among the houses and shops of a loftily straggling suburb, where pleasant lanes and paths are fast in the way of disappearing before the builder. In those remoter quarters, one could get lodgings more easily at the height of summer, when the sea front of Hastings is crowded with holiday-making visitors.

The characteristic climate here is mild, and on the sea front, hemmed in by steep cliffs, will be found relaxing. But thanks to its situation, Hastings has the advantage of offering a variety of temperature, for the visitor who desires more bracing air has only to seek the heights and the long lines of terraces and villas which spread inland. While at High Wickham, St. Mary's Terrace, St. Michael's, the heights above Ore, or the uplands behind St. Leonards, one may feel oneself almost on a Yorkshire coast, the deep valleys in Hastings become sometimes oppressively warm, and the shut-in stretches of the front are suitable to the most delicate lungs, being, says Sir James Clark, "more effectually sheltered from north and north-east winds than any other place frequented by invalids on the coast of Sussex"—an advantage attested by countless convalescent homes and hospitals established here, chiefly at the St. Leonards end. It is also comparatively little subject to fogs, and the rainfall, by no means high on this coast, is soon carried off by the porous sandy soil. Hastings has a high record of sunshine, with a yearly range of temperature comparatively small for our island. The prevailing wind is from the south-west, which, blowing along with a high spring tide, may prove somewhat alarming, as in the great New Year's Day storm of 1877, when the pier was damaged, and the houses at the west end of the Marina were invaded by a flood that beat in doors and windows like brown paper.

The drainage and water-supply are medically certified as good. The bathing is also to be well spoken of on the whole, the shore being shingly, and in some parts rather steep, with patches of sand and rocks uncovered at low tide; but there is hardly room enough for a children's playground; and this does not make a good family watering-place. Machines are to be found at several points which, as often happens, have to stand at high tide rather too near the Esplanade for strict propriety. At each end there is a strip where men may bathe quite *al fresco* "in the fearless old fashion." The shelf of shingle hidden behind the fishing-boats at Hastings makes one of the best and most popular bathing-places on the coast, its position freeing it from all restrictions, while for a copper or two the unprepared stranger may be provided with a towel and a plank to stand on, and a boat is kept ready in case he gets into trouble. The free bathing ground at the west end beyond "Bo-Peep" is not quite so recommendable. At both, in rough weather, caution is necessary, as has been shown of late by some unfortunate accidents.

So much for the general features of Hastings. It is now time to describe it more particularly, conducting the stranger from the *Railway Station*, which stands on a height, a few minutes back from the sea.

Down the curved line of *Havelock Road*, we pass to an open space, junction of several streets, where the *Albert Memorial Clock Tower* may be called the Charing Cross of the place. Here start nearly all the suburban omnibuses and driving trips; and the shore in front of it is the port of the pleasure yachts that carry so many landsmen to sea in fine weather; this part of the beach, when tide permits, forming also an open-air theatre, occupied by various bands of minstrels, and other entertainers. The *Queen's Hotel* here overlooks the sea.

The chief street running inland hence is the *Queen's Road*, where, on the right, are at once found the *Post Office* and the *Theatre*, then a little farther, on the other side, the *Town Hall* at one corner of a spacious *Cricket Ground*, often used for athletic displays. *Station Road*, turning off along the cricket ground, would take us back to the railway. The *Public Rooms* are at the corner of *Havelock Road*.

Following a short line of busy street eastward, or

going round by the sea front, we soon reach the three-sided oblong called *Wellington Square*, rising up the foot of the *West Hill*, crowned by its castle ruins, the face of which now crowds in the line of houses so close to the shore that there is no more room for a back street, except where *Pelham Crescent* exalts itself on the cliff, with the classical façade of *St. Mary's Church* in the centre, where the services are of an old-fashioned type, suggested by the structure. *Breed's Place* leads us so far; then we must take the open *Marine Parade*, till Hastings finds room for throwing out streets of business into the next valley. Turning up *George Street*, the chief of these, past the *Coastguard Station*, here almost swamped by landlubberly houses, we soon reach the *Lift* by which lazy legs may be carried up the hill, else ascended by way of *Wellington Square* or *Castle Road*, or at various points on the other side.

The *West Hill* is to a large extent laid out as a recreation ground, with seats and paths across the turf. At the back of it stands one of the elevated quarters of Hastings, where *Plynlimmon Road* and *St. Mary's Road* are main thoroughfares. There are fine views in all directions, especially from the *Castle* ruins so conspicuous on the edge of the cliff, 300 feet above the sea (admittance 3d., closed on Sundays).

Hastings Castle dominated the old town, its principal entrance necessarily on the land side, where the portcullis groove and the hooks for the gate hinges may yet be examined. The castle area occupied about an acre and a quarter. The south side was 400 feet long; the east side 300 feet long, with a fosse, and a massive wall strengthened by three semicircular towers. To the west, both a square and a circular tower are still standing, and a doorway which formerly opened into the Royal Chapel of St. Mary, a Transitional Norman structure, 110 feet long, with a nave, chancel, and aisles.

The manor was bestowed by King William on the Count of Eu, who may have erected the castle. It remained in the hands of his descendants until the middle of the 14th century, when, according to tradition, it was consumed by fire. Adela, daughter of King William, presided here as Queen of Love and Beauty at the first tournament celebrated in England. The castle now belongs to the Earl of Chichester.

St. Clement's Caves on the east side of the hill make a curious spectacle, though the romantic fables about them do not seem justified by fact. (Admission 6d.; and the caves are sometimes illuminated for music and dancing.) The late Mr. Campbell Dykes, a resident at St. Leonards, wrote an interesting article on these caves, which appeared in the *Illustrated London News* of 1st June 1895, just at the time of his death. They are said to have been formed by digging for sand, but haunted by smugglers only in juvenile imagination.

The Ladies' Parlour is the name given to a hollow near the top of the Lift.

On the sea front below the Castle, either by the Parade, or more shadily by George Street behind, we pass across the mouth of the next valley into which so much of old Hastings is closely packed, where we must look out for the remaining patches of quaint antiquity. At the other side, the narrow *High Street* turns up to the left, leading out of the town as the *Old London Road*. On the left of it stands *St. Clement's Church*, one of venerable antiquity and containing some relics of the past worth inspection, besides two French cannon balls embedded in its tower. Farther on, to the right, where the road opens out, is the Roman Catholic *St. Mary Star of the Sea*, that owes its erection largely to Mr. Coventry Patmore, the venerable poet, who lives close at hand. To the east of this again on the road, presently converging with the line of High Street, we have the fine church of *All Saints*, in the graveyard of which lies George Mogridge, known as a writer for the young under the name of "Old Humphry." The *Hydropathic* is at the head of this valley, about a mile back from the sea.

All Saints Street, farther east, runs parallel to the *High Street*, at the foot of which is the *Fishmarket*, and here begins the picturesquely cramped end of Hastings dear to artists. The sturdy fisher-folk of this port preserve from more adventurous days a good deal of robustness and individuality of character, their peculiarities being kept up by close intermarriages, while there is an occasional infusion of foreign blood brought by daughters of Heth from beyond the Channel. They number some thousands, supported by an extensive industry.

The "Dutch" fish auction sales, which attract crowds of a fine morning to this part of the beach, reverse the usual order of procedure : one of the owners begins by naming his price, and steadily decreases, calling out monotonously, probably sixpence less each time, while men, women, and children are all watching and listening eagerly, until some one bids, who then becomes the purchaser.

Now the gay line of Parade loses itself in the cottages and alleys of a fishing village, by which we come under the chalk face of the *East Hill*, throwing into relief the rich effects of black and brown below, where tall tarred tanning-sheds stand sentinel over spread-out nets ; and on the other side of the broad beach is drawn up a long rank of heavy bottomed craft, the difficult launching of which makes a spectacle for idle excursionists. Here is the men's bathing-place, whence ladies should keep aloof, passing behind by the narrow *Rock-a-nore Road* below the cliff to the substantial groin or breakwater, that brings Hastings abruptly to an end, all but its *Sewage Works*.

The shore beyond is rough, and not lightly to be taken as a road, though at low tide the cliffs are well seen from below. These crumbling banks are rather dangerous, honeycombed by recesses, one of which, known as *Butler's Cave*, was made by an old man who had many visitors to his happy family of fowls, pigeons, rabbits, etc.

To the Downs on the *East Hill*, we can safely ascend by a staircase through the fishing village, or one a little way up All Saints Street. The top, its treacherous edges fenced off, makes another spacious and airy pleasure ground. Here are the *Golf Links*, and towards the farther side traces of a great encampment, believed by some to have been William the Conqueror's ; but his first camp was more probably on the hill where we started from the railway station. To this central point let us now return to follow Hastings westwards into **St. Leonards.**

From the *Memorial Clock*, we can either take the sea front past *Robertson Terrace*, or follow *Robertson Street* behind, which is perhaps the chief line of shops. To the right go off *Trinity Street* and *Claremont*, short converging streets largely taken up by the *Brassey Institute*, that contains, besides an Assembly Room, the *Corporation Reference Library* and the *Hastings Museum*, both open free. The *School of Science and Art* is also located here.

Robertson Street bends round upon the Parade, where the latter again forms a single line of shops, large hotels, and lodging-houses under another hillside, for the most part as yet unbuilt on. By *White Rock*, beside the *Hospital*, we can ascend to *St. Margaret's Road*, running along the face of this hill to the grounds of the Catholic *Convent of All Souls*, and its adjacent church. Below is the Band Stand, on the broadest and most frequented part of the Parade, formed by the roof of the *Baths*, which may claim with reason to be the best of their kind in England. There are large sea-water swimming baths, both for gentlemen and ladies (1s.), besides Turkish and other baths.

Beyond the Baths, runs out the *Hastings Pier*, over 900 feet. The *Pavilion* at the end of it contains the largest assembly room in the town, noted for the entertainments given here, as, for instance, a pantomime at Christmas, with no charge for standing room beyond 2d. paid for admission to the pier. From the pier, in summer, a pleasure steamboat makes trips to *Eastbourne*, to *Dungeness*, round the *Sovereign Lightship*, and to farther points of the Channel.

A very genteel stretch of the Parade, known as *Eversfield Place*, brings us to the opening of *Warrior Square*, which, like Wellington Square, is not a square, but an oblong, very spacious and stately. Behind it lie the *Warrior Square Station*, and *St. Paul's Church*, a handsome modern structure with rich internal decorations.

West of Warrior Square comes the thickest built part

of St. Leonards, answering to the valley quarter about the High Street of Hastings. At this end also we find a *London Road* running inland as the chief thoroughfare, on the left of which is soon reached *Christ Church*, noted for its high services. Near the bottom, the Parade was till recently spanned by that arch marking the St. Leonards boundary. Then the sea front is broken by one isolated block of houses known as the *Colonnade*, past which the promenade takes the style of the *Marina*, part of it, on the shore side, forming another colonnade.

To a high and extensive suburban quarter behind, *Maze Hill* runs up beside the *St. Leonards Public Gardens*, a sheltered retreat, shady and flowery in a somewhat old-fashioned style. West of them are the *Archery Gardens* (*tennis, croquet*, etc.), open only to subscribers or at the charge of 6d. for a visit. The *Gensing Pleasure Grounds*, some way up the London Road, also have a tennis ground, and are open free.

We have now followed the Marina as far as the new *St. Leonards Pier*, which seeks to rival the gaieties of its Hastings neighbour, but as yet, it is feared, with less success. A peculiarity of it is the Pavilion being near the shore end, leaving room for a carriage road, on which one may drive out to sea.

Between the Pier and the *St. Leonards Gardens* is an open space where the *Assembly Rooms* stand behind the *Royal Victoria Hotel*. St. Leonards has a *West Hill* of its own, to which we can here ascend by a sloping road to find the height being fast covered with large buildings in the new-fashioned style, their redness and variety making a contrast to the stuccoed monotony of the *Marina* below. This long Parade ends at last with a triangular strip of public garden, beyond which pretentious terraces still make incursion into the more humble quarter that used to be known as "Bo-Peep," but is now styled *West Marina*, to just its altering circumstances.

We cannot undertake to conduct our readers through the labyrinth of suburbs stretching out to *Silverhill* and *Hollington* behind St. Leonards, and to *Ore* behind

Hastings for a distance almost equal to the length of the town. But we must not pass over the *Alexandra Park*, which winds its way for a mile through a serpentine valley at the back between those elevated lines of suburb. It is best reached by passing up *Queen's Road* from the Memorial; ten minutes bring us under the railway, when the gate of the park is seen on the left. Through it runs a small stream, utilised to form sheets of water in the lower part. The upper division, narrowing at the top under *Shornden Wood*, contains a rarely gorgeous show of flowers, a great change from the swampy wilderness one used to traverse here. This upper part might also be gained by passing by the Electric Light Works, the smoke from which is voted a nuisance on neighbouring heights, then over the *Cornwallis Estate* behind the station, and taking a footpath into the valley, with fine views over the farther ridges; but the building going on here hinders us from giving precise indication. Near the top of the park, on the left-hand side, is a chalybeate well. A *Spa* for dispensing the same water will be found at a corner of *St. Helen's Road* on the right of the lower park; but this institution does not seem to flourish, as if Hastings visitors needed no medicament beyond the air and the sea.

From the reservoir above the Park, a path leads up the valley, past the waterfall of *Old Roar*, once one of the local lions, but now it roars you as gently as any sucking dove, besides being enclosed in private grounds. Gaining the ridge, and sweeping round to the left, where again the builder is playing havoc with old landmarks, we could strike the high road from Battle, which divides at *Silverhill*, on the right going down into St. Leonards as the *London Road*, on the left as the *Bohemia Road*, descending through the quarter oddly named " Bohemia," to come into Hastings, latterly under the name of *Cambridge Road*, at the Memorial Clock, where so many ways debouch.

The visitor who wanders inland must take care to keep himself related to one of those main lines : the *Old London Road*, in the valley between East and West Hill ; the *Queen's Road*, in the next valley westward ; the *Bohemia Road* and

The Albert Memorial, Hastings

Robertson Street and Carlisle Parade, Hastings

the new *London Road* converging on the heights behind St. Leonards.

Omnibuses run frequently from the *Memorial Clock* to the *Park*, to *Silverhill*, to the high part of *Ore*, and to other points in the suburbs. Besides longer drives, of which we will speak presently, there are in summer brakes plying as often as they can be filled (1s. 6d.) for *Fairlight Glen*, which is *the* short trip to be taken here, by one or other way, best done on foot along what is the most beautiful if not the grandest part of the Sussex coast. The driving road goes inland by Ore, and is up-hill most of the way.

Fairlight Glen opens some 2 miles along the cliffs eastward. We go out over the East Hill; and if we escape flying golf balls, may chance to come upon a more alarming peril in the first steep dip, should red flags proclaim that rifle practice is going on across it. The bottom of this glen is so deep that once there, one would be quite safe; but the path by the edge of the cliff seems hardly safe under such circumstances. In any case, the farther ascent makes a trying pull, and one does not go far wrong in turning up by the path along the west side of **Ecclesbourne Glen**, which leads on through a dark wood of coppice and wind-twisted trees, a fine retreat on a hot day, where, as well as at the back of Fairlight Glen, a refreshment booth does thriving business. This makes a short roundabout, the path running on to the right of a reservoir into a road, where, taking at once the stile on the right and a cart track along a field, one gets back to the cliff path a little before the opening of Fairlight Glen.

Much frequented as it is, and spoilt of late years as some tell us, this deep wooded recess makes a lovely piece of greenery. One can cut across its mouth by another steep up and down, or take the course of the stream at the bottom to pass up to the head by the *Dripping Well*, where the water plashes over the rock under a fine beech tree; or go round the upper part by a circuitous path touching the road from which those who drive enter at the top. The path through the woods here (*guide-post*) joins the cliff path on the next broken headland, below which we can get down to the *Lovers' Seat*, associated in local legend with a tale of old true love that did not run smooth, and still often turned to account by young couples in like case—let us hope theirs will be a happier story!

Below, the subsidence of the cliff has brought about a chaos prettily overgrown with coppice-wood, an uncommon feature so near the sea; but it is difficult to get down to most parts of this broken shore, and still more to get up again, while in winter we can answer for having had trying experience of floundering through one of those seaside jungles. The Lovers' Seat makes the usual goal of Hastings rambles, and one might well spend a whole afternoon in scrambling through the shady recesses of the glen. But we can keep the cliffs on to *Pett Level*, and thus make our way to Winchelsea in half a dozen miles or so farther; or we might turn up inland to **Fairlight Church**, whose high tower makes such a conspicuous beacon at the top of the Down (over 500 feet), to rest here for the view from its finely situated churchyard, which contains some interesting tombstones.

From the church there are various pleasant ways home, a distance of 3 or 4 miles to this side of Hastings. We might follow a path to the high-standing *Coastguard Station*, and so back by the cliffs; or taking the road along the high ground behind, a path to the left would soon bring us down to the back of Fairlight Glen, whence a road runs straight into Hastings behind the East Hill, with the choice of diverging to the cliffs either through Ecclesbourne Glen or over the Golf Links. This road, the shortest, comes down into Hastings above *All Saints' Church*. The road from Fairlight Church (marked by telegraph posts) would take one a little farther round, to descend through *Ore*, where an omnibus might be found to abridge the way; but it is pleasanter than the last-mentioned route, especially if one make a turn off it on the right, a little way past the lodge behind Fairlight

EXCURSIONS FROM HASTINGS

Glen, where presently a path leads to the top of a height nearly 600 feet, once crowned by a mill, now by an enclosed circle of turf and a huge seat for enjoying the fine views in every direction. Thence a lane drops back into the road we have left, or we may bear on into the high road from Rye, which joins this one at Ore. Even if the way be lost in these suburbs, so long as one keeps down hill and to the left, the line of the London Road is bound to be reached.

The coast-line beyond St. Leonards is by no means so attractive, and walking along the bank of shingle here makes hard work. The favourite hour's walk at this end is inland to **Hollington**, where Charles Lamb for once gave way to enthusiasm about its little "church in the wood," a wood that seems like to suggest St. John's Wood before long, so fast are the suburbs growing about it. Hence one might make another hour's divagation to **Crowhurst** (5 miles), a fine old church with a venerable yew-tree to show, whose years are fondly counted in thousands. From Crowhurst a longer round might be taken through *Sidley Green* and *Bexhill* to St. Leonards, or by the back of Hastings to come in through *Ore*. But, having thus indicated the resources of the immediate vicinity, we proceed to visit the whole district in various directions, as can so well be done from Hastings.

EXCURSIONS FROM HASTINGS

Every morning in the season, about 10.30, brakes start from the *Memorial Clock*, bound on trips to some extent fixed by the days on which houses like Battle Abbey are open to the public. We cannot answer for the permanency of the enclosed programme, which was in force last year, but inquiry will make certain. Shorter drives, as to Bexhill and to Fairlight Glen, can be had more frequently.

Monday. Winchelsea, through Guestling (18 miles drive) . . . . 3s.
Tuesday. Battle Abbey and *Normanhurst* (21 miles) . 4s.

HASTINGS

Wednesday { *Winchelsea* and *Rye* (24 miles) . . 4s.
{ *Bexhill* and *Sidley* (12 miles) . . 2s.
Thursday. Bodiam *Castle*, through Sedlescombe (25 miles) . . . . 4s. 6d.
Friday. *Hurstmonceaux*, through Battle and Ashburnham Park (28 miles) . . . . 5s.
Saturday. Short drives in the vicinity . . . 2s.

TO RYE AND WINCHELSEA

For Rye (11 miles) may be taken either the drive, as above, or the London and South Eastern Railway towards *Ashford Junction* (for Dover, Ramsgate, etc.), which goes out at the back of the east end of Hastings, the first station being the suburb of *Ore*. The railway then sweeps round over extensive flats, once covered by water, and still, in parts, hinting at a marshy character. On the right (9 miles) appears the wooded bank crowned by *Winchelsea*, the station being about a mile to the north. Leaving this to be visited on our way back, we cross the flats where they open to the sea, and presently come in sight of *Rye*, an eminence thickly covered with red roofs and weather-worn walls, at first sight strongly suggesting a Dutch town, a resemblance carried out by the windmills, the dykes, and the green level dotted with cows. The old-world charms of this place have of late brought it much into note with artists, while its airy situation recommends it as a summer resort, so that it now attracts not a few sojourners as well as visitors for the day. The river **Rother** here (to be distinguished from the *Rother* of West Sussex) forms the boundary between Sussex and Kent; then beyond this come the flats of Romney Marsh; and Kent ends in the promontory of Dungeness, beyond Rye New Harbour.

RYE

Hotels: *George* in High Street; *Cinque Ports* (C.), near station; *Temperance Inn*, High Street.

Boarding-Houses: *Western House*, Winchelsea Road; the old *Mermaid Inn*, in the town, has recently been turned into a boarding and lodging house with studios for artists.

Mr. Louis Jennings, in his *Field Paths and Green Lanes*,

describes Rye and Winchelsea as "the Spithead and Portsmouth of their day," and says that "nothing more recent than the Cavalier's cloak and hat and ruffles should be seen at Rye." At one time the sea came up to the walls, but owing to its gradual subsidence, the harbour is now about 2 miles off, at the present mouth of the Rother, after its junction with the Brede and the Tillingham. The old town suffered much from attacks of the French in the 14th century, and also from pestilence. A great number of Huguenots took refuge here in 1572 after the massacre of St. Bartholomew's Day, and others in the next century, exiled by the Revocation of the Edict of Nantes. Among them was one family named *Jacques*, from which came Samuel Jeake, the antiquary, who published a work on the Charters of the Cinque Ports. Rye was also the birthplace (1579) of John Fletcher, the celebrated dramatist, best known by his association with Beaumont in the annals of English literature, and of Dr. Isaac Todhunter, the mathematician (1820).

Those wishing to make the best of an afternoon visit to this venerable haven that was, are advised to proceed as follows. On leaving the station turn to the left along *Cinque Ports Street*, which presently brings one up to the *Landgate*, still in very fair preservation, the only one of the old portals now remaining. Passing between its massive towers we mount up to *High Street* by a railed bank looking over the *Salts*, the town recreation ground, to the *Rother*, which may be seen winding its flat way to the sea 2 miles off. On the other side, beyond the bridge, a steam tramway has just been opened to the new harbour, and this would take us down for a bathe. It is quite evident how the sea once came right up to this hill, before which the *Rother* unites with the *Brede*.

Entering the *High Street*, we see at once how this is no common town, clustered closely with such fine effects of colour, quaintness, and that mellowing of time which can best be expressed by the French word *fruste*. Some of the houses set off their ancient countenances by a pretty show of flowers blooming in front. Twisting and dropping through the maze of side streets, too short for losing one's way anywhere, the chief thoroughfare, under the name of the *Mint* at its farther end, comes down upon the bridge by which we must cross for Winchelsea. But let us meanwhile return to its beginning near the *Landgate*.

On the right, presently, the Temperance Inn stands at the corner of *Conduit Hill*, a little way down which will be seen the chapel of a *Monastery*, dating from the 13th or 14th century. This building, after being turned to various base uses successively, is now again a place of religious service, with a difference, being used by the Salvation Army.

A little way along the other side of High Street comes the *George Hotel*, a hostelry of ancient note. Here we may turn up to the *Church*, whose low tower forms the crown of the town. Jeake describes it as, in his day, the finest church of Kent or Sussex, except the cathedrals; and it makes still a striking if somewhat composite edifice, in length about 160 feet. The chapels on either side the chancel have been restored, that of *St. Nicholas* being used as a school, and *St. Clare's* for separate services. There are several interesting memorials; and the church clock is noticeable for its age and its long pendulum.

Near the south-east corner of the churchyard, on the edge of the height, rise the remains of the *Ypres Tower*, once an important fortress, and till lately used as a prison. The level space beside it is still known as the *Gun garden*, from having made part of the fortifications up to this century. Here we get another view over the flats to the sea.

Passing along the south side of the churchyard, almost at the western end of the row of houses will be noticed one whose pointed arch hints at its having once made part of a religious edifice, though it is now a private residence. This is believed to be the oldest building in the town, the only one surviving two destructive conflagrations in the 14th and 15th centuries.

WINCHELSEA

Holding on past this house, we get into *Watch Bell Street*, which leads to another open view, now looking over towards Winchelsea on its opposite height. The road thither will be seen running below; but to get to it we must bend round to the right, or regain the *High Street*, which leads down to the bridge. Half-way between Rye and Winchelsea appears **Camber** or **Winchelsea Castle**, a solid structure even in ruins suggesting a conglomeration of Martello Towers.

It is 2 miles to Winchelsea by the military road, the left side of which is shut in by a provokingly high hedge that hides the view over to Camber Castle and the sea. On the other side of this hedge is a broad piece of water, where the *Brede* has been adapted as part of the *Royal Military Canal*, available here for boating and bathing, while its elevated banks appear to be designed as defensive works in case of need. The road bends along the course of this water to cross it by a bridge, beyond which we must double back to mount the height on which Winchelsea is almost lost among greenery. It has plenty of room now, and even in its palmy days it could afford to be built spaciously on a regular plan, whereas Rye, we see, had to huddle itself together for safety within narrow bounds.

WINCHELSEA

(*New Inn* and Refreshment Rooms.)

Though Winchelsea be now a mere village, it once, like Rye, was an important place, as may be guessed from the solid and picturesque pile of the *Strand Gate*, through which we enter at the top of the ascent, where it frames for us a fine picture of Rye. A fragment of the *Landgate* will be seen on the road to *Udimore*; and three-quarters of a mile out towards *Pett*, one is surprised to come on another lonely arch, the *New Gate*, showing the former extent of the place. But before it flourished on this site, Old Winchelsea occupied another some way to the south, from which it was driven by encroachments of

Hastings from East Hill

Fishing boats on the beach at Hastings

the sea. New Winchelsea was built by Edward I. in a style to match the greatness of its haven. A plan will be found in Parker's *Domestic Architecture of the Fourteenth Century*. Several times it was attacked, and more than once burned by the French, from whose assaults it might have recovered, but the rapid withdrawal of the sea and destruction of its harbour were not to be contended against. When, in 1573, it was visited by Queen Elizabeth, she christened it "Little London"; perhaps ironically, for then not more than sixty families remained in the town, and it has never since held up its head. It is, as Wesley called it in 1790, when he preached his last sermon under a widespreading ash tree adjoining the west side of St. Thomas's Church, the "poor skeleton of ancient Winchelsea." But up to 1832, it returned two members to Parliament, one of them Henry Brougham, the reformer of such anachronisms.

The village now stands roomily grouped round the green on which is displayed its fine old church. "Rye Church," says Mr. Basil Champneys in his *Quiet Corner of England*, which makes a good guide-book here, "is a conglomeration of schemes and styles, mostly of a rude vernacular character: Winchelsea Church is an almost ideal gem of uniform character and of exquisitely studied detail." It is doubtful whether this church was ever completed. The transepts were begun, and there are some traces of the nave, but the work was probably stopped by the misfortunes which fell on the town.

The style is Early Decorated, and from its purity deserves particular examination. Remark the fidelity of the sculptured foliage; the curious corbel heads; the rich foreign tracery of the side windows; the piers of Bethersden marble and Caen stone; the sedilia in the chancel (recently restored); the Perpendicular English windows; and the light and airy three-bayed choir. In the south aisle is the *Alard Chantry*, originally the Chapel of St. Nicholas, where are particularly to be observed the noble *Alard* tombs — one to Gervase Alard, Admiral of the Cinque Ports, 1303, showing a recumbent cross-legged effigy under a noble arched canopy, adorned with heads of Edward I. and Queen Eleanor. When Millais was lodging here he sketched this tomb for his picture,

WINCHELSEA

"Safe from the Battle's Din," in which an infant is placed for security on an old tomb. He invited Thackeray to come down and see the district, as the latter did, whereby originated his novel *Denis Duval*, the plot of which is laid in this vicinity. The companion tomb, with some fine foliaged ornamentation, and a canopy resembling that already alluded to, is to Stephen Alard, grandson of the above, and Admiral of the Cinque Ports in 1324. In the north aisle is the Chantry of John Godfrey, died 1441, and Maline his wife. There are also the three canopied tombs, *temp*. Henry III., with effigies of a mailed templar, a lady, and a young man, robed. In the floor of the chancel is inserted a brass for a priest, died 1440. The triple gable of the chancel, luxuriantly shrouded in ivy, is connected with the ruined transept walls. Over the porch are the arms of Winchelsea.

On the south side of the place lies the *Friars*, to which admission is obtainable only on Mondays. The present house was erected in 1819, when the old Franciscan monastery was taken down. The beautiful ruins of the *Chapel of the Virgin*, founded in 1310, have happily escaped. "The Friars" was the residence, in 1780, of two daring robbers, George and Joseph Weston, one of whom was actually appointed churchwarden of Winchelsea, and both brothers living here, under assumed names, on the plunder acquired in their daring excursions, were held in much repute. After robbing the Bristol mail they were detected, apprehended, and one of them was hung. James, the novelist, in one of his best romances, has made good use of these facts.

From Winchelsea one may return to Hastings on foot by several ways. The high road makes 9 miles, passing by **Icklesham**, with an ancient church, then **Guestling** (4 miles from Hastings), where one might turn aside to examine its church, a Transitional Norman building, restored in 1885, the tower surmounted by a low spire, standing about 300 yards from the road. The *Ashburnham Chantry* is divided from the south aisle by three pointed arches; the nave from the north aisle by two Norman aches with chevron mouldings. In the vestry stands an old richly-carved "Flanders chest."

Or it would be a little longer to make for the shore

below Winchelsea, and follow it by road and path. But as the first part of this route takes us by the less interesting stretch of *Pett Level*, a middle way may be suggested that is agreeable throughout and still capable of a little variation. Go out towards *Icklesham*, passing through the *New Gate*, and keep the road making a bend round towards **Pett**, whose graceful church spire becomes a landmark after 3 miles or so, and another mile of winding lane brings us to the village. The church, rebuilt 1864, contains some good stained glass windows in memory of the Young family.

Here take as the next beacon *Fairlight Church*, a tall tower on the most conspicuous part of the coast. By *Pett Church* goes off a footpath that would lead over the hollow to two trees seen standing on the shoulder of the height a little below Fairlight Tower, and thence it would be easy to gain the cliff path. But if one follow the road (which would lead round into Hastings by Ore), one had better take the turning to the left, where a guidepost directs to Fairlight Church, very visible as it is on the opposite ridge. This road leads over the hollow in front of Fairlight Hall, its last turn to be cut off by a footpath; and if the steep is rather trying, almost impracticable for cyclists, henceforth all the way is down hill by one or other of the ways suggested in our excursion to *Fairlight Glen*.

Were it preferred to make an inland round by the course of the *Brede* and the flats north of the railway, this would carry one up by **Udimore** (3 miles from Winchelsea), which has a small ancient church; then to **Brede**, lying between the river and the road through Udimore, to the right of which is *Great Sowden Wood*, containing a large heronry. South of this, on the slope of a gentle acclivity, stands the quaint old manor-house of *Brede Place, temp.* 14th century, now made use of as a farm, but anciently the residence of the Attefords, from whom it passed, early in the reign of Henry VI., to the Oxenbridges. One of this family, Sir Goddard, who about 1530 made considerable additions to the mansion, is traditionally reported to have lived upon human flesh, with a particular relish for that of infants. Neither bow and arrow, nor axe, nor sword, nor spear, could slay this redoubtable giant, but some of the country folk about here succeeded at length in making him drunk, and sawing him in half with a wooden saw! His house, about a century ago, was tenanted by a gang of smugglers, who, by inventing strange sights, and uttering unearthly noises, contrived very effectually to secure it to themselves. The hall, and a room beyond it, with their Caen stonework and enriched windows, should be examined.

The *Church* is equally worthy of notice. The Brede chantry was enlarged and repaired by Sir Goddard Oxenbridge, who chiefly employed French workmen, and their skill and fancy may be admired in the window traceries and the foliated decoration of the doorway. Observe his monument, and effigy in Caen stone.

From Brede one might make one's way home by **Westfield** (5 miles from Hastings), a pleasant village with an Early English Church. This would be a round of some dozen miles.

BODIAM CASTLE

To this show-place, lying near the edge of the county, north of the Rother, we might go by Brede and the village of *Northiam* beyond. But the shorter road, and that taken by the excursion brakes, is through the picturesque and picturesquely situated **Sedlescombe**, containing some old timber-fronted houses, and a noticeable Early English Church. Here there was a Roman iron work.

On the left bank of the Rother, which a little below becomes the border of Sussex, stands **Bodiam Castle**, one of the most perfect moated fortresses remaining, though (as may be traced by its construction) it was erected at a period when the recent invention of artillery was impairing the usefulness of such defences. A deep fosse, filled with water, and fed by the Rother, encircles it. A round tower fortifies each angle of the area (165 feet by 150); the great gateway, approached by a causeway, is conspicuous on the north side; and in the centre of the other sides rise up stout square towers. The central court is 87 feet by 78 feet. Over the main gateway observe the armorial bearings of the Bodiams, Dalyngrudges, and Wardeuxs—into whose hands the castle successively passed. The outer portcullis may still be examined, and the tourist will find much to interest him in the remains of the hall, chapel, and kitchen.

A charge of 6d. is made for admission to this ruin, which, so far as the shell goes, is one of the best preserved in England, and vies with Hurstmonceaux as the finest in Sussex. *Bodiam Church* at the other end of the village is an Early English building of some interest.

The nearest railway station to Bodiam (on the South-Eastern Railway between Hastings and Tunbridge Wells) is **Robertsbridge** (*i.e.* Rother's Bridge), under 4 miles from Bodiam by path along the river (apt to be swamped in wet weather), and somewhat farther by road through **Salehurst**, under *Silverhill*, a bold ascent overlooking a "whole horizon of the richest blue prospect," which warmed Horace Walpole to something like enthusiasm, though elsewhere his mood is to proclaim Sussex "a great damper of curiosity." *Robertsbridge* itself (Inn: *The Old George*) is a small cluster of old-fashioned, red-brick houses, intermingled with some brand-new villas. On the river bank, in one of those sweet sequestered valleys, so dear to the Cistercian monks, moulder the scanty ruins of a Cisterian abbey, founded, in 1176, by Alured de St. Martin. The site of the chapel is still discernible.

While here one might hold on to the next station, **Etchingham**, which could be reached on foot over Silverhill; this, as well as the road by the station, goes rather out of the way, making the distance quite 4 miles, but with fine views; and a shorter footpath by the Rother might be taken in dry weather.

Etchingham Church is one of the most interesting in the county, dedicated in honour of the Assumption of the Virgin Mary (a rare English dedication). Its general character is Decorated, with a massive square tower, a staircase turret, a roof of unusual height, and windows ornamented with rich flamboyant tracery. The founder of the church was one Sir *William de Etchingham*, died 1387, to whom there is a brass in the chancel (much injured), and an inscription which may be compared with that on the Black Prince's tomb at Canterbury. An enriched canopy overhangs a brass to the later Sir *William*, died 1444, his wife, and son, and the south aisle is adorned with an Etchingham helmet. Other memorials and the ancient font will be noticed. The church was tastefully restored in 1851. A noble yew flourishes in the graveyard.

About 3 miles to the west, on the hills, stands **Burwash** (*de Burghersh*, pronounced *Burrish*), a large and busy village, with an interesting church, enlarged and restored in 1856, noticeable for containing "a curious specimen of the iron manufacture of the 14th century, perhaps the oldest existing article produced by our Sussex foundries. It is a cast-iron slab, with an ornamental cross, and an inscription in relief. In the opinion of several eminent antiquaries, it may be regarded as unique for the style and period. The inscription is much injured by long exposure to the attrition of human feet. The letters are Longobardic, and the legend appears, on a careful examination, to be—

"ORATE P. ANNEMA JHONE COLINE (or COLINS).
Pray for the soul of Joan Collins."

From Robertsbridge, or from Etchingham (through Burwash), we may visit **Brightling** (13 miles from Hastings by road through Battle or Ashburnham; 4 miles from Robertsbridge station). The elevated situation here affords magnificent views over the Wealds of Kent and Sussex and the English Channel; occasionally, it is said, even the French coast may be seen. It is a favourite resort of tourists from St. Leonards and Eastbourne. On the highest point of this elevation (646 feet) an Observatory has been built; admission free, and telescopes are kept for visitors. It is said to be visible from the neighbourhood of London, and the lofty columnar landmark near it must be of great service to the mariners of the Channel. The site of the ancient fire-beacon is curiously named "Brown's Burgh." *Brightling Church* is an ancient stone building dedicated to St. Thomas à Becket.

From Brightfield one could descend to **Mountfield** station, the next after Robertsbridge on the way back to Hastings. Gypsum, from which plaster is worked, was discovered at *Netherfield*, in this parish, during the borings in a vain attempt here to reach the Palæozoic rocks.

BATTLE ABBEY

Half-way to Robertsbridge on this line is **Battle**, 6 miles by road or rail (Hotels: *George* (C.), *Star*). This is a little town of some size, where many come on pilgrimage to the scene of the great fight, included by Sir Edward Creasy amongst the *Fifteen Decisive Battles in the History of the World*. A view of the Abbey gateway—"one of the finest gate-houses belonging to a religious establishment that remain in England"—may be caught from the railway. The Duchess of Cleveland is the proprietor, and it is open to the public on *Tuesdays*, tickets being obtained at the stationer's shop opposite to the gateway.

Before we enter into any minute examination of Battle Abbey, it will be advisable to put together a few details of the great victory which its founder designed it to commemorate. Fuller particulars than we can here afford will be found in Professor E. A. Freeman's *History of the Norman Conquest* (vol. iii. chap. xv.), who describes the battle as "The most memorable day in the history of our island since England became one kingdom." For the assistance, however, of those who cannot spare time to study Mr. Freeman's stirring pages the following epitome may be of service:—

The Battle of Senlac (or Hastings).—In 1066 the English King, Edward (afterwards named "the Confessor"), had fallen thoroughly under Norman influence, and being childless had, about 1051, promised his cousin, Duke William, the succession to the English crown. Harold, Earl of the West Saxons, and son of the powerful Earl Godwin, was brother-in-law to the weak-minded King Edward. About 1064 Harold, with some of his relatives, started from Bosham in Sussex for an expedition in the Channel, but being wrecked on the opposite coast at Ponthieu, was betrayed to Count Guy, the Lord of the district. This fact coming to the knowledge of his over-lord William, the latter ordered Harold's release, and entertained him hospitably, though he was virtually a prisoner. It was alleged that Harold then took an oath over concealed relics to recognise William's right of succession, and to marry his daughter. The true facts are very obscure; and, even if such an oath were taken, it is obvious that William knew the oath would never be kept, and, moreover, it is to be observed that the English crown did not strictly descend, but was in the gift of the people.

Harold returned to England, and on the death of Edward the Confessor, on 5th January 1066, the King indicated his wish that Harold should succeed him. The Assembly unanimously elected Harold as King, and he was crowned a few days later. "Harold was not," says Mr. Freeman, "a Dionysios, a Cæsar, a Cromwell, or a Buonaparte, whose throne was reared upon the ruins of the freedom of his country. . . . To Harold the Crown of England was freely offered in all its glory and greatness."

As soon as the news reached William, he resolved on an invasion of England, and having obtained the support of the Norman barons and some princes of neighbouring territories, the summer of 1066 was occupied in preparing the fleet. The number of vessels, as stated by various writers, ranges from 696 to 3000, though possibly in the smaller number only the larger vessels are reckoned, and the number of men also varies from 14,000 to 60,000. William, under the plea of Harold's perjury, obtained the Pope's blessing and a consecrated banner. In August 1066 the fleet was ready to sail, and had collected at Varaville, at the mouth of the Dive. An adverse wind delayed the expedition, till William, on 12th September, with the aid of a west wind, proceeded to St. Valery. At last, on Wednesday, 27th September, the longed-for south wind blew, a start was made, and on the morning of 28th he landed at Pevensey. A hostile resistance was expected, and the soldiers landed in battle array, the first to set foot on the English shore being their leader. He accidentally fell, and this raised a cry of grief at the evil omen, but his ready wit interpreted the fall as "taking seisin of the earth of England in his hands." Not a blow was struck, for Harold was in the north, and the English fleet had been disbanded. The archers scoured the shore, the knights mounted their horses, and Pevensey was occupied. One day only was spent here, and on the next they moved, "probably along the line of a Roman road," to Hastings, which became William's headquarters and the centre of operations. "It was William's object to bring Harold down to the sea-coast to tempt him to an attack on the Norman camp, or to a battle on the level ground," and a systematic harrying of the country round took place, traces of which are distinctly found in Domesday twenty years later.

About 1st October Harold, celebrating at York his victory over the Norsemen at Stamford Bridge, received news of the Norman landing and ravages. He hastily marched to London, arriving about a week after the landing at Pevensey. A messenger from William claimed the throne and threatened war. He was sent back by Harold, who accepted the challenge for the coming Saturday. Six days were spent in collecting men, and Harold set out on Thursday, 12th October. "The consummate generalship of Harold is nowhere more plainly shown," says Mr. Freeman, "than in his plan of this memorable campaign." The Normans anticipated an attack, but Harold did not intend this. He knew Sussex well, and no doubt selected the place in which he would give battle. His march was straight to the intended spot, and lay along the great road from London to the south coast. He halted on a spot commanding that road, and also the road east from William's position, and the camp was pitched on the heights of Senlac, about 7 miles from Hastings.

The hill of Senlac, now occupied by the abbey and town of Battle, is the last spur covered by the great Andredes-weald. Of a peninsular shape, stretching from east to south-west, and joined by a narrow isthmus to the high ground to the north, it commands the ground of hill and marsh between itself and the sea, which was doubtless in an October of those days a mere quagmire.

On this hill Harold entrenched himself, surrounding it on all sides by a palisade, with a triple gate of entrance, defended on the south by an artificial ditch. The Royal Standard was planted just where the ground begins to slope to the southeast. The hill was occupied on Friday, and next day the battle was fought. After a speech by William, the Normans marched to the hill of Telham, here getting their first sight of the English. William vowed that if God gave him the victory he would, on the spot where the English standard stood, raise a mighty minster to His honour. A monk named William ("the Faber," or Smith) stepping forward, begged the Duke to dedicate the building to St. Martin, to which he agreed.

The Normans then marched on in full battle array, and in three divisions. The infantry were first exposed to the attack, as a charge of the knights up the slope would have been madness. The English, from the King downwards, were on foot, and ranged so closely together in the thick array of the shield-wall that, while they only kept their ground, the success of an assailant was hopeless. To the south-west of the hill beyond the isthmus seem to have been placed the less trustworthy portions of the English army, the recent levies, mostly without armour. At nine o'clock the battle began, and the Norman infantry vainly attempted to break the palisade, being met with showers of stones and javelins. The knights now came forward, but the long-handled English axes cut down horse and man, and rank after rank pressed on in vain. A panic seized the Bretons, forming the Norman left, who, thinking William slain, fled, pursued by some reckless defenders of the English right, till William, removing his helmet, addressed them, and turned them on their pursuers, who were cut to pieces. A second and more desperate attack ensued, and the Duke himself pressed towards the standard, when he was unhorsed by Gyrth, Harold's brother. William rose to his feet, and attacked Gyrth, who fell crushed under the Norman's iron mace, and at his side fell his brother Leofwine. The fight continued fiercely, William mounting another horse, and a third when that was killed. Still the fight went ill for the Norman. Observing the success obtained in the first flight, he ordered a feigned flight of his left, producing another headlong charge of the English right, who were at once attacked, with terrible slaughter. The western and most accessible part of the hill was thus left open, and the Normans ascended without having to cut through the palisades. Desperate struggles and personal encounters then went on all over the hill, but after a time the English resistance slackened.

As evening drew on, William ordered his archers to shoot upwards, and a shower of arrows fell on the defenders of the standard. One pierced Harold's right eye, and he fell. Four Norman knights attacked him, one drove through his shield and stabbed him in the breast, another smote him with the sword below the fastenings of his helmet, a third pierced his body with his lance, and the fourth cut off his leg. The standard was beaten to the ground, but while daylight lasted the fight continued. Under cover of darkness the light-armed English fled, and being pursued by the Normans down the steep slopes to the north a great slaughter ensued, no quarter given on either side.

When night closed in, the Conqueror returned to the hill, and pitching his tent where the English standard had stood, knelt and gave thanks to God for his victory. Wolves, not then extinct in Sussex, feasted on the bodies of the slain. On the Sunday morning, after a long search, the mangled corpse of Harold was discovered by his mistress, Eadgyth Swanneshals, and refused Christian burial by the Conqueror, who directed it to be wrapped in a purple robe and buried on the sea-coast under a cairn of stones, whence some years later the remains were translated to Waltham Abbey.

That portion of Battle town which now lies east of the church is called the Lake, and sometimes *Sanguelac*, or Senlac—*i.e.* "the lake of blood,"—so named, it is said, by the Conqueror, "because of the vast sea of gore there spilt." It was called *Sant Lache*, however, long before the Battle of Hastings. In like manner, the springs of chalybeate water hereabouts which form the sources of the Asten, derived their redness, in popular tradition, from the blood of the slaughtered Saxons.

The Conqueror's vow was fulfilled by the erection of the stately pile of the Abbey of *St. Martin de Belli loco*—that is, on the actual place of the battle ; the church being consecrated on 11th February 1094, during a visit of William Rufus to Hastings. The Abbey was richly endowed by the Conqueror, and became the centre of a town and district 3 miles in diameter, known as a "leuca" or "lowey," over which the Abbot enjoyed a special and peculiar jurisdiction. It was peopled with monks from the Benedictine monastery of Marmoutier, in Normandy, who in time fell into the shameful demoralisation that brought ruin on so many noble foundations.

At the time of its dissolution, the site was conferred upon Sir Anthony Browne, and by his descendant, the fourth Lord Montacute, was sold to Sir Thomas Webster. Sir Anthony Browne converted the southern part of the monastic buildings into the present stately mansion.

Battle Abbey.—Fronting the street still stands, in excellent preservation, the *Gate-house*, Late Decorated in style, and probably erected by Abbot Bethynge, *temp.* Edward III. The house nearest to it, on the west side, was the Pilgrims' *Hospitium*, and is called the *Almonry ;* the range of buildings to the right, now in ruins, was long made use of as the *Town Hall*.

Passing within the entrance, we first inspect the *Abbots' Hall* (only shown occasionally, when the family are not in residence), 57 feet by 30 feet, very lofty, and timber-roofed. It was in this hall (according to an old story) that on taking possession in 1538 Sir Anthony Browne was holding a house-warming when a monk crept in and pronounced his curse on the knightly spoliator of the Church ("the Curse of Cowdray"), declaring that "by fire and water his line should come to an end, and perish out of the land." The prophecy had a singular fulfilment last century, for in the autumn of 1793 the eighth Lord Montacute was drowned in a mad attempt to shoot the falls at Laufenburg on the Rhine, while about the same time his beautiful seat at Cowdray, in West Sussex, was totally destroyed by fire.

Next come the *Dormitory*, now converted into a corridor

and bedrooms; and the *Beggars' Hall*, a vaulted apartment underneath. Then we visit the terrace, traditionally reputed to have been the *Banqueting-room*, overlooking the scene of the great battle. Below it are eight vaults, each of them 29 feet by 14 feet, which had been magazines for provisions and fuel.

Viewing afterwards the east front of the splendid pile, we remark its nine arches enriched with Perpendicular tracery. On the site of the flower-garden stood the conventual *Church*, whose foundations were excavated in 1817, and the apse of whose crypt and the bases of its columns still remain uncovered. "*Siste, viator; heroa calcas!*"—the high altar stood on the spot where Harold fell.

> "Here rose the dragon-banner of our realm;
> Here fought, here fell, our Norman-slander'd king.
> O Garden blossoming out of English blood!
> O strange hate-healer Time! We stroll and stare
> Where might made right eight hundred years ago;
> Might, right? ay good, so all things make for good—
> But he and he, if soul be soul, are where
> Each stands full face with all he did below."
>
> Prologue to Lord Tennyson's drama, *Harold*.

The Early English *Refectory* (or *Frater's House*), with its lancet-windows and buttressed walls, and the vaulted rooms beneath it, must next be visited. One of the latter, the largest, has been called the *Scriptorium*, or *Library*, and among the books which Leland found here was Prior Clement of Llanthony's highly edifying treatise on *The Spiritual Wings and Feathers of the Cherubim*.

The Battle Abbey roll of Norman knights, from which Duke William, it is said, called over his band of followers on the morning of the fight—probably a later fiction, or, at least, compilation, of the Battle monks—was preserved in the monastery until the Dissolution, and afterwards removed to Cowdray, to be destroyed in the great fire.

For more complete particulars of the Abbey (with a plan distinguishing the ancient and modern portions), the visitor may consult a valuable little Guide, published by the Duchess of Cleveland, anonymously, under the initials "C. L. W. C."

Battle Church is Transitional Norman in style, with a few Decorated additions. It contains a little stained glass; and in the chancel stands the white marble tomb of Sir *Anthony Browne*, with recumbent effigies of that gallant knight and his wife *Alis*. Observe the brasses for a knight in armour, died 1425; Sir *W. Arnold*, died

1435 ; *Robert Acre,* died 1440 ; and *John Wythines,* died 1615, Deans of Battle.

The brakes from Hastings usually pass round by **Normanhurst Court** (3 miles west of Battle), the palatial residence of Lord Brassey ; also open on Tuesdays, by tickets to be obtained at the Royal Victoria Library, St. Leonards. A charge of 1s. is made, going to local charities. The house contains many valuable modern paintings, and a collection of curiosities brought from all parts of the world in the famous voyages of the *Sunbeam.*

Beyond Normanhurst westward extend the grounds of **Ashburnham Place,** a brick mansion containing some relics of Charles I., but not shown to the public. There is an open way, however, across the beautiful park, with its woods and dells, offering rich prospects.

Hurstmonceaux and *Pevensey Castles* are also favourite excursions from Hastings, the way taken being by Ashburnham ; but they have come within the radius of Eastbourne, to which we refer the reader. To one place in this direction, however, we will here conduct him, since it bids fair to be soon a rival or a suburb of St. Leonards. This is *Bexhill*, which may be reached along the shore, or by road or rail ($2\frac{1}{2}$ miles from the *Marina*), or by field path turning off close to the *Bull Inn*, near the scanty remains of the old church of **Bulverhithe**, beyond St. Leonards.

BEXHILL

Hotels : *Sackville, Marine,* first class, on the shore ; *Bell,* in the village ; *Devonshire* (C.), at the station.

Four or five miles from Hastings station westward, on the London, Brighton, and South Coast Railway, nearly all trains are now bound to stop at a rapidly risen resort as yet describable as divided into two parts, which, however, will soon run together, if building goes on at its present rate. The old *Bexhill* is a quiet and picturesque village on the hill above the station ; its chief features an ancient church much restored, that contains a Scandinavian slab referred to Anglo-Saxon times, and did contain a remarkable east window of painted glass, which Horace Walpole managed to " convey " to his collection at Strawberry Hill ; then a large new *Convalescent Home*, a walnut tree said to be the most venerable in Sussex, and the *Manor House*, a fine restored mansion, containing some very ancient fragments, once the Palace of the Bishops of Chichester, now occupied by the Sackville family, through whose courtesy the grounds, and the cricket field appertaining, go far towards the entertainment of Bexhill visitors.

Bexhill on Sea, lying mainly on the other side of the railway, is a new and smart watering-place, whose success has raised the population to over 5000 in the season. It might be called the Broadstairs of Hastings and Eastbourne, serving as a sort of chapel-of-ease to these overgrown resorts ; but as only a mile separates the outlying houses of Bexhill and St. Leonards, the day is not far distant when the one seems like to annex the other as a dependent.

The attractions of Bexhill are an airy situation, a capital shingly beach, with stretches of sand at low water, occupied in force by tents and bathing machines, and a long esplanade which, on the St. Leonards side, borders a stretch of excellent golf links that are no doubt the chief factor in this sudden prosperity. On the other side, visitors have access to *Egerton Park*, containing a sheet of water, tennis ground, etc. Here the coast is not very interesting, soon going off into the Pevensey flats and low banks studded by Martello Towers. On both sides are the remains of a submarine forest to be visited at low tide.

Bexhill, laying itself out to be a quiet family watering-place of distinction, does not encourage the boisterous forms of amusement in favour with trippers ; but it has a new band-stand, a good *Institute*, with reading-room, billiards, library, etc., and *Assembly Rooms* for entertainments ; and now it is adding to its attractions an ambitious Kursaal. Cricket and tennis flourish here as well as golf. Sailing trips may be taken, and driving excursions inland to the lions of the vicinity, *Pevensey Castle*, *Battle*, etc. Drainage and water supply are looked to ; and nearly all the houses being new show a bright *tout ensemble* in contrast with the stucco period of sea-side architecture. On the whole, this is a place paterfamilias ought to know about.

The country around is said to abound in chalybeate springs, which some day may give a new development to Bexhill. What of it strikes the eye at first sight from the railway station is not markedly picturesque; but there are some pretty nooks to be sought for, such as *Chantry Lane*, and a good deal of fine woodland behind the village. A pleasant stroll is to **Little Common** (*Wheatsheaf Inn*), from which one might turn to the right to come back to Bexhill by the *High Woods* and *Sidley Green*, or make a longer round to *St. Leonards* through *Crowhurst*, which, again, might be lengthened by holding on from Little Common to **Hooe** (10 miles from Hastings), where there is an ancient church with a remarkable window said to resemble that taken from Bexhill, and thence tramping by *Ninfield* and *Catsfield*, the latter 9 miles from Hastings, and an hour's walk from *Battle* station. The beauty of this district is highly praised both by Mr. Louis Jennings and by Mr. J. J. Hissey in his *Holiday on the Road*.

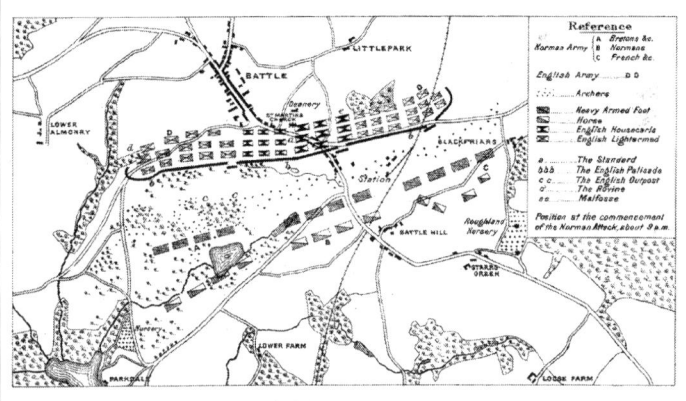

BATTLE OF HASTINGS

West Street, Rye

'A good catch'

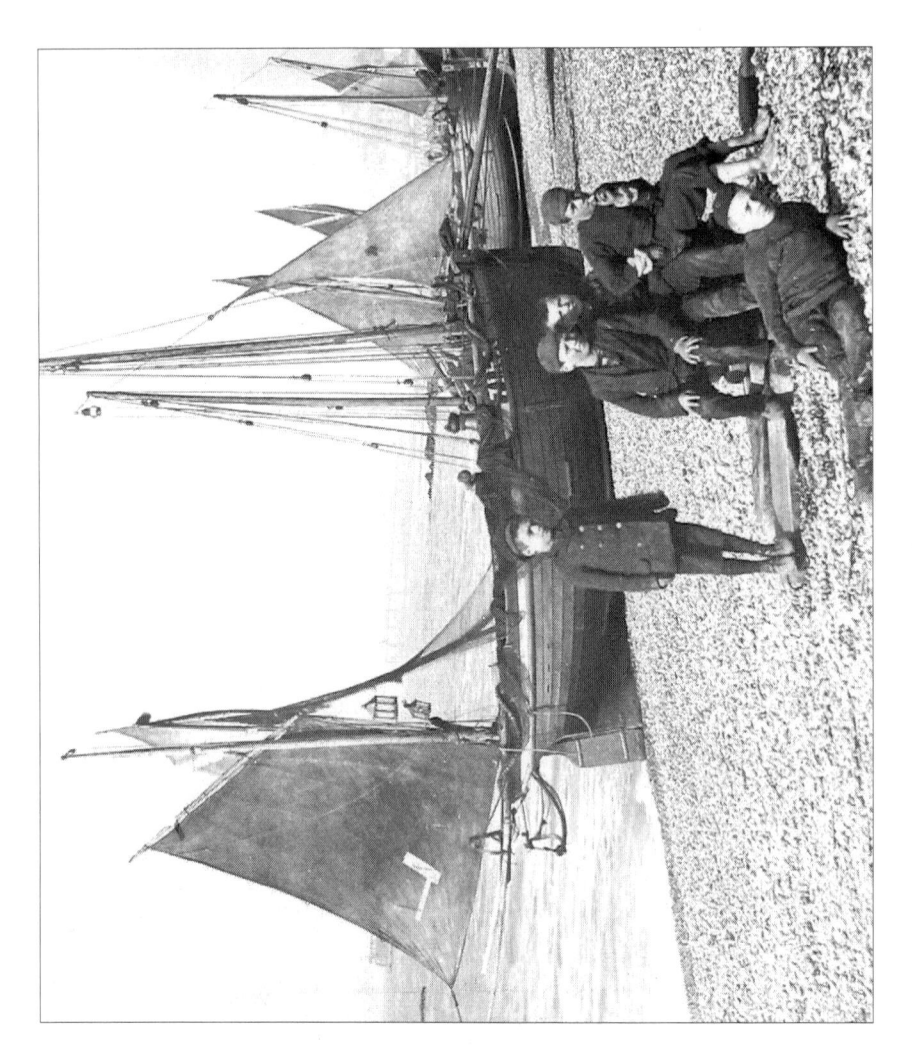

On the beach at Hasting

A German U-Boat on Hastings Beach, 15th April, 1919

The East Hill Lift, Hastings

Andrew Gill: I have collected historical photographs and optical antiques for over forty years. I am a professional 'magic lantern' showman presenting Victorian slide shows and giving talks on early optical entertainments for museums, festivals, special interest groups and universities. Please visit my website '**Magic Lantern World**' at www.magiclanternist.com

My booklets and photo albums are available from Amazon, simply search for the titles below. If you've enjoyed this book, please leave a review on Amazon, as good ratings are very important to independent authors. If you're disappointed, please let me know the reason, so that I can address the issue in future editions.

Historical travel guides
New York
Jersey in 1921
Norwich in 1880
Doon the Watter
Liverpool in 1886
Nottingham in 1899
Bournemouth in 1914
Great Yarmouth in 1880
Victorian Walks in Surrey
The Way We Were: Bath
A Victorian Visit to Brighton
The Way We Were: Lincoln
A Victorian Visit to Hastings
A Victorian Visit to Falmouth
Newcastle upon Tyne in 1903
Victorian and Edwardian York
The Way We Were: Llandudno
A Victorian Visit to North Devon
The Way We Were: Manchester
A Victorian Guide to Birmingham
Leeds through the Magic Lantern
An Edwardian Guide to Leicester
Victorian and Edwardian Bradford
Victorian and Edwardian Sheffield

The Way We Were: North Cornwall
A Victorian Visit to Fowey and Looe
A Victorian Visit to Peel, Isle of Man
Doncaster through the Magic Lantern
The Way We Were: The Lake District
Lechlade to Oxford by Canoe in 1875
Guernsey, Sark and Alderney in 1921
East Devon through the Magic Lantern
The River Thames from Source to Sea
A Victorian Visit to Ramsey, Isle of Man
A Victorian Visit to Douglas, Isle of Man
Victorian Totnes through the Magic Lantern
Victorian Whitby through the Magic Lantern
Victorian London through the Magic Lantern
St. Ives through the Victorian Magic Lantern
Victorian Torquay through the Magic Lantern
Victorian Glasgow through the Magic Lantern
The Way We Were: Wakefield and Dewsbury
The Way We Were: Hebden Bridge to Halifax
Victorian Blackpool through the Magic Lantern
Victorian Scarborough through the Magic Lantern
The Way We Were: Hull and the Surrounding Area
The Way We Were: Harrogate and Knaresborough
A Victorian Tour of North Wales: Rhyl to Llandudno
A Victorian Visit to Lewes and the surrounding area
The Isle of Man through the Victorian Magic Lantern
A Victorian Visit to Helston and the Lizard Peninsula
A Victorian Railway Journey from Plymouth to Padstow
A Victorian Visit to Barmouth and the Surrounding Area
The Way We Were: Holmfirth, Honley and Huddersfield
A Victorian Visit to Malton, Pickering and Castle Howard
A Victorian Visit to Eastbourne and the surrounding area
A Victorian Visit to Aberystwyth and the Surrounding Area
The Way We Were: Rotherham and the Surrounding Area
A Victorian Visit to Castletown, Port St. Mary and Port Erin
Penzance and Newlyn through the Victorian Magic Lantern
A Victorian Journey to Snowdonia, Caernarfon and Pwllheli
Victorian Brixham and Dartmouth through the Magic Lantern
Victorian Plymouth and Devonport through the Magic Lantern
A Victorian Tour of North Wales: Conwy to Caernarfon via Anglesey
Staithes, Runswick and Robin Hood's Bay through the Magic Lantern
Dawlish, Teignmouth and Newton Abbot through the Victorian Magic Lantern

Walking Books
Victorian Edinburgh Walks
Victorian Rossendale Walks
More Victorian Rossendale Walks
Victorian Walks on the Isle of Wight (Book 1)

Victorian Walks on the Isle of Wight (Book 2)
Victorian Rossendale Walks: The End of an Era

Other historical topics
The YMCA in the First World War
Sarah Jane's Victorian Tour of Scotland
The River Tyne through the Magic Lantern
The 1907 Wrench Cinematograph Catalogue
Victorian Street Life through the Magic Lantern
The First World War through the Magic Lantern
Ballyclare May Fair through the Victorian Magic Lantern
The Story of Burnley's Trams through the Magic Lantern
The Franco-British 'White City' London Exhibition of 1908
The 1907 Wrench 'Optical and Science Lanterns' Catalogue
The CWS Crumpsall Biscuit Factory through the Magic Lantern
How They Built the Forth Railway Bridge: A Victorian Magic Lantern Show

Historical photo albums (just photos)
The Way We Were: Suffolk
Norwich: The Way We Were
The Way We Were: Somerset
Fife through the Magic Lantern
York through the Magic Lantern
Rossendale: The Way We Were
The Way We Were: Cumberland
Burnley through the Magic Lantern
Oban to the Hebrides and St. Kilda
Tasmania through the Magic Lantern
Swaledale through the Magic Lantern
Llandudno through the Magic Lantern
Birmingham through the Magic Lantern
Penzance, Newlyn and the Isles of Scilly
Great Yarmouth through the Magic Lantern
Ancient Baalbec through the Magic Lantern
The Isle of Skye through the Magic Lantern
Ancient Palmyra through the Magic Lantern
The Kentish Coast from Whitstable to Hythe
New South Wales through the Magic Lantern
From Glasgow to Rothesay by Paddle Steamer
Victorian Childhood through the Magic Lantern
The Way We Were: Yorkshire Railway Stations
Southampton, Portsmouth and the Great Liners
Newcastle upon Tyne through the Magic Lantern
Egypt's Ancient Monuments through the Magic Lantern
The Way We Were: Birkenhead, Port Sunlight and the Wirral
Ancient Egypt, Baalbec and Palmyra through the Magic Lantern

Copyright © 2021 by Andrew Gill. All rights reserved.
No part of this book may be reproduced or used in any
manner without written permission of the copyright owner.

Contact email: victorianhistory@virginmedia.com

Printed in Great Britain
by Amazon